THE BOOK OF ANT RECORDS
AMAZING FACTS AND FEATS

Katja Bargum

illustrated by Jenny Lucander

translated by B.J. Woodstein

ORCA BOOK PUBLISHERS

NORTH AMERICA

SOUTH AMERICA

This book is about ants and their amazing abilities. The world of ants is swarming with records because ants have superpowers.

You might be wondering, "Superpowers? What do you mean? Ants are tiny. They can't set records, can they?"

But actually, ants have tons of secret talents. Thanks to those talents, ants can live anywhere in the world. They can live in the desert at 120 degrees Fahrenheit (50 degrees Celsius), inside an acorn, under the ground, in the treetops or in your home.

They can build anthills that are taller than a grown-up human being. Ants can even make a living nest by holding on to one another and creating a ball out of ant bodies.

Ants have existed on earth for millions of years, ever since the time of the dinosaurs. There are approximately 20,000,000,000,000,000 ants on the planet—that's 20 million billion ants!

If they all were to stand in a row, that line of ants would go back and forth to the sun 200 times!

Not bad, right? Are you ready for more ant records? Turn the page!

The Best Sense of Smell

Have you ever looked really closely at an ant? Up close, the ant looks like an alien.

But what do we humans look like to ants? To them, it isn't actually so important how we look but rather how we smell. Ants experience the world through their sense of smell.

The body of an ant is like a scent factory. It is made up of parts that detect and release smells.

Jaws serve as both hands and mouth for an ant. Ants can use their jaws to carry big loads, bite enemies and taste food.

Inside an ant's body there are tons of glands that create different scents. Ants from the same anthill have the same smell. When two ants meet, they sniff one another to see if they recognize each other. If one of them smells foreign to the other, they fight.

Ants can even smell with their feet!

When an ant finds food, she releases a scent trail with her bottom as she returns to the ant colony. The ant rubs her bottom against the ground so the scent sticks. That way, other ants can follow the trail to find the food.

The Largest Ant Colony

Just like humans, ants are social animals who live and work together in a society. An anthill is like a city where all the ants have their own tasks.

The world's largest naturally occurring ant colony is on the Japanese island of Hokkaido. It is a big city with thousands of anthills. The anthills cover an area as big as 400 football pitches. If you were to walk from one end of their city to the other, it would take you an hour.

These mound ants go back and forth between the nests and feel at home in all of them. This sort of ant society is usually called a *supercolony*.

Which home should I choose tonight?

The largest anthill in the world was built by the **MOUND ANTS OF HOKKAIDO.**

Most of the ants who scurry about on the ground are female. They are called *workers*, because they work basically all the time and take care of almost everything that happens in the anthill. Usually all the workers have the same parents.

A worker ant works for her whole life, from the time she's born. When she's young, she works inside the anthill. She takes care of her little siblings and cleans the nest. When she gets older, she starts going out, getting food and defending the anthill from enemies.

The Least Common Ant

The least common ant in the anthill is the queen ant. You don't see her often, not even if you are an ant researcher. The queen hides deep inside the mound. Usually there is just one queen per anthill.

She is the most important ant in the mound, because she is the one who lays the eggs so new ants are born. During her lifetime, the queen can have many millions of babies. She is the mother of all the ants in the anthill.

The queen is bigger than the workers and has a big bottom, so there's room for all her millions of eggs. The workers get food for her, take care of her and sniff her. They can tell from the queen's smell if she is healthy and can lay lots of eggs. If the queen stops smelling the way a good queen should, the workers stop taking care of her and start laying their own eggs instead.

The least common ant is the **ANT QUEEN.**

Hi, Mom!

Mmm, she smells great!

Hi, number 138,224!

The Cleverest Ant

When a queen is still a young princess, she has wings. She uses them to fly from the anthill she was born in, and then she mates with male ants from other nests. After that she lands on the ground and pulls off her wings.

The muscles she used for flying are now needed for the heavy work of building a new nest.

Look, the boys are coming!

In the late summer, you might see a princess ant creeping around, looking for a place to dig her nest. The princess digs a hole in the ground or in an old stump, then lays her eggs.

The eggs hatch into little workers, who immediately begin taking care of their mother. The princess has turned into a queen and can finally lean back and relax.

But some princesses are cleverer than that. In this picture, a mound ant princess has sneaked into another ant species' nest, killed the nest's queen and taken power for herself. She didn't have to go to the trouble of digging.

This stump is already taken!

Ha ha!

The cleverest ant is the **MOUND ANT PRINCESS.**

PAIN POINTS

The prize for the worst ant sting goes to the **BULLET ANT**.

4	bullet ant	spider wasp
3	yellow paper wasp	harvester ant
2	honey bee	bulldog ant
1	fire ant	sweat bee

The bullet ant of South America has the worst sting. When she stings, it feels like being shot by a pistol, and the pain lasts for hours.

How do we know that it's the worst sting? Well, the American researcher Justin Schmidt tested being stung and bitten by a bunch of insects, and he gave the bullet ant four out of four possible pain points.

Over the course of millions of years, mound ants and many other ants have lost their ability to sting, and instead they bite when it's necessary. Rather than venom, they produce a chemical called formic acid that they shoot onto their enemies. You can smell the formic acid if you sniff an anthill or hold your hand over a mound when the ants are out. But be careful! Too much formic acid can damage your skin!

Watch out! I'm shooting!

15

The Angriest Ant in North America

There are around 1,000 types of ants in North America. Most don't attack humans, but the little fire ant is an angry type. She has a sting like a wasp, and when she sticks you with it, it can feel like you've been burned.

Fire ants build mounds in soil and live underground, especially in open, sunny areas. So look out the next time you have a picnic or play in a field!

Western thatching ants are a type of mound ant native to North America. They don't have stingers and that's lucky, because they are found in all types of habitats, including grasslands, prairies and forests. They get their name from the roof—called a thatch—that they build over their nest using small twigs, fir needles, grass and other plant materials.

I don't like being disturbed, so stay away!

The angriest ant is the **FIRE ANT**.

Look out—the boot monster is coming!

Carpenter ants look more dangerous than they actually are. They're the biggest ants in North America, and their queen can grow as long as a dime. But the carpenter ant doesn't have a stinger and prefers to chew on wood rather than people. She gnaws paths through the wood and builds her nest there. Usually a stump works well as a home, but sometimes the carpenter ant might build a nest in a house wall.

The little cornfield ant is a softy. She doesn't sting or bite, but she does love jam sandwiches. That's why she sometimes comes into homes in the spring, when there isn't as much to eat outdoors. Cornfield ants are one of the most abundant ants on the continent.

The Strangest Ant Food

Ants eat lots of different things, including other small animals, plants, seeds and mushrooms. One of the strangest ant foods is pee from aphids, which are small, soft-bodied insects that eat plant sap. Many ants around the world live on aphid pee. For example, shiny sugar ants and mound ants milk the sweet liquid out of the aphid's bottom. The aphids are like the ants' milk cows. If you see ants climbing up a tree trunk, they are surely on their way to their aphid herds, which live on the leaves or branches of trees.

Ants take good care of their "cows." Ladybugs like to eat aphids, and if a ladybug gets too close to the aphid flock, the ants will chase it away.

If the aphid isn't milked often enough, it can drown in its own pee!

But the strangest menu is the one Dracula ants prefer. They suck blood from their own larvae—their own babies! The larvae are a sort of kitchen cupboard for the ant colony.

If a Dracula ant gets really hungry, she makes a hole in one of the ant larvae and sucks up some of the bodily fluids. Luckily, the larvae don't die. They still develop into totally normal adult ants.

The prize for the ant who eats the strangest food goes to the **DRACULA ANT**.

No, sister, don't eat me!

The Most Frightening Ant

In South America there's a type of ant whose jaws look like pitchforks. Guess what we call these ants? Pitchfork ants, of course! They use their pitchforks to grasp and stab millipedes, their prey. First an ant stings a millipede to paralyze it. Then, holding the millipede firmly between her jaws, like a sausage on a skewer, the ant uses her legs to peel off the millipede's sticky hairs and eats it while the prey is still alive.

The most frightening ant is the **PITCHFORK ANT**.

The Fastest Ant

The fastest ants in the world live in the desert. During the day the sand gets so hot that you could fry an egg on it. Ants who are out looking for food have to hurry as quickly as they can to get back into their cool nest.

A desert ant can run a distance that is equivalent to 100 times her body length in just a second. If you could run that fast, you'd get from one end of a major-league baseball field to the other in just a second.

To find her way home to the nest again, the ant keeps track of where the sun is in the sky. The ant also counts her steps all the time. That's not easy, since she can take 40 steps per second!

The fastest ant is the **DESERT ANT**.

432, 433, 434, 435, 436, 437, 438, 439...

The strongest ant is the **AZTECA ANT**.

The Strongest Ant

Azteca ants use an interesting hunting strategy. They line up side by side along the edges of the underside of a leaf. They use their claws to grip to the leaf like Velcro. When prey such as a moth lands on the leaf, the ants use their jaws to grab their prey's legs and hold it down, working together to capture it. Each ant can hold 5,000 times her own weight. If we were as strong as these ants, we could carry a jumbo jet in our jaws while hanging upside down by our toes.

Sometimes ants use their strength to carry one another. Many mound ants live in different anthills in the winter and the summer. When they move out to their summer home, they often carry each other.

Thanks for the ride!

Lazybones.

Ants have this super strength because they are super small. Since they are so light, they require very little energy to move their own bodies. That's why they can use all their muscles for lifting, carrying and dragging. If you and your friends were shrunk down to the size of ants, you'd also easily be able to carry a friend in your outstretched arms!

The Best Farmer Ants

The ant world's best farmers are the leafcutter ants. They have enormous fungus gardens in their homes. They cultivate the fungus fields with leaves that they slice into pieces and chew into a sticky mess. Then they eat the bits of the fungus that stick up out of the soil. The whole colony lives almost entirely on fungus.

Sometimes the fungus gets diseased. Then the ants spread out medicine in their fields. The medicine is a sort of antibiotic that grows on the ants' own skin.

The leafcutter ant princesses take a little bit of fungus with them when they move out from the nest. When a princess has found a good place to start her colony, she plants the fungus in the nest's roof.

The best farmer ants are the **LEAFCUTTER ANTS**.

The Cleanest Ant

Ants are very clean animals. If you've ever seen a cat wash itself, then you know what ants do. They lick their bodies and use their legs for the parts they can't reach with their mouths. They have small brushes and combs on their legs to get rid of dirt and bits of debris.

Some mound ants also gather resin from fir trees. Resin kills bacteria, especially when it's mixed with formic acid. A piece of resin from an ant mound is a real health bomb!

Ants use many different types of cleaning products in their nests. A mound ant shoots out formic acid from its bottom and spreads it out over the nest and the larvae. Formic acid is a liquid that can kill bacteria. That is why it has also been used to preserve animal feed. The Finnish researcher A.I. Virtanen discovered this method, which earned him the Nobel Prize in Chemistry in 1945.

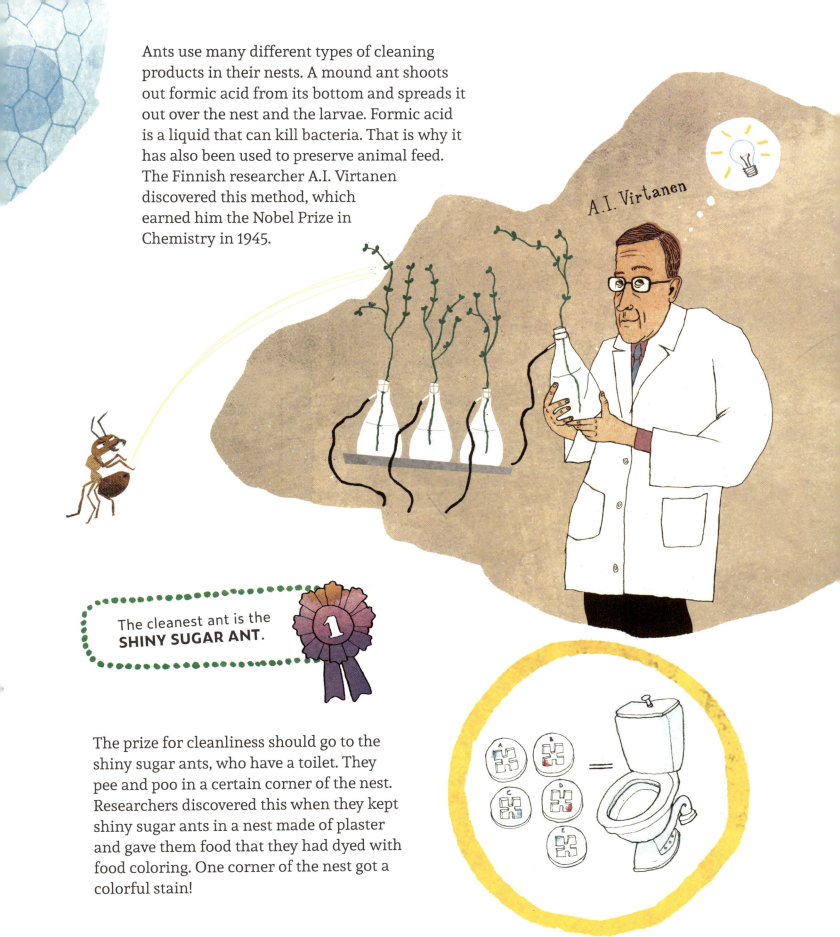

The cleanest ant is the **SHINY SUGAR ANT**.

The prize for cleanliness should go to the shiny sugar ants, who have a toilet. They pee and poo in a certain corner of the nest. Researchers discovered this when they kept shiny sugar ants in a nest made of plaster and gave them food that they had dyed with food coloring. One corner of the nest got a colorful stain!

The Toughest Soldier Ants

In Borneo there's a type of carpenter ant who builds her nest in tree trunks in the rainforest. The nest has two kinds of workers. The big workers make sure that no foreign ants come into the nest, and they do this by functioning as living doors.

They cover the entrances to the nest with their heads, which are shaped like corks.

The toughest soldier ants are the **CARPENTER ANTS FROM BORNEO.**

The smaller workers defend the nest by exploding like bombs.

If a foreign ant comes too close to the nest, the worker grabs the intruder in an iron grip. She pulls her stomach muscles together so hard that the back of her body splits. Out of it flies a yellow, slimy and venomous liquid that kills the enemy.

Nooo! Slime!!!

The Sneakiest "Ant"

If you were to go through an entire ant mound, you'd find hundreds of other species that live there as guests or parasites. Some just use the anthill as a home, but others steal the tasty food the ants bring in or even eat the ants' own larvae.

Among the sneakiest tricksters of ants are the blue butterflies. The larva, or caterpillar, of a blue butterfly attracts common red ants because it sweats out a substance that smells like the red ants' own larvae. The common red ant, believing that the smell is coming from an ant larva that has gotten lost, carries it into her nest. Inside their house, the colony feeds the larva of the blue butterfly. Instead of being grateful, the caterpillar also gobbles up the ants' own larvae. In the end, it gets bigger than the red ants and turns into an adult butterfly.

I'm just a little ant baby!

The sneakiest "ant" isn't an ant at all—it's the **BLUE BUTTERFLY**.

The Biggest Appetite for Ants

There are some animals who almost exclusively eat ants. You will recognize the greediest of these creatures by their names, which often start with *ant*.

Anteaters live in North and South America. Scaly anteaters, or pangolins, live in Africa and Asia. And spiny anteaters, or echidnas, live in Australia. All of them have strong forelegs and big claws, which they use to dig deep into the ant nest's passageways. They have narrow noses and long, sticky tongues, which they use to fish out the ants.

But they don't have any teeth, since they can eat the ants whole. They also have thick fur or hard skin, which protects them when the annoyed ants try to sting or bite them.

The prize for the biggest appetite for ants goes to the **ANTEATER**, **PANGOLIN** and **ECHIDNA**.

I have the longest tongue!

No, I do!

Look at mine!

In North America, woodpeckers and bears, among many other animals, like ants a lot. They particularly like to eat them early in the spring, when there isn't so much other food to eat.

People can also eat ants. In Finland, in earlier times, people ate ant pupae, which are ants in the stage of development between a larva and an adult ant. In Latin America, people toast leafcutter ant princesses and eat them like popcorn. In Asia, a spicy sauce is made from weaver ants.

The Best Source of Warmth

Ants are cold-blooded animals. That means their body temperature depends on the temperature around them. When it's warm, ants are warm and can move quickly. When it's cold, they get stiffer and slower.

In the summer the worker ants air out the anthill so the temperature stays the same no matter the weather. They also move the larvae and pupae around often. Ant babies always need to be warm and comfortable so they can grow quickly.

Cloudy again. I can't go anywhere!

In the winter the ants gather together into tight groups in the earth, as far down under the mound as they can go. As long as the ground around them doesn't freeze, the groups of ants can survive the winter.

When the spring begins to let a little warmth into the earth, the ants slowly start to move and warm up their muscles. Their movements make the anthill so warm that you can see patches of snow that have started to melt on top of the mound.

The prize for the ants' best source of warmth goes to the **ANTHILL**.

The Longest-Lived Ant

How long an ant can live depends on the type of ant. Queens win by a big margin. Researcher Lotta Sundström studied the queen from a colony of the narrow-headed ant, on an island off Finland's coast. The queen ant lived for 30 years! That makes her one of the most long-lived insects in the world.

The longest-lived ant is the **QUEEN OF THE NARROW-HEADED ANTS**.

Lotta Sundström

The Farthest-Traveled Ant

Ants have come to live in new places around the world by traveling along with humans. When people send plants, seeds and vegetables from one place to another, an ant or two can easily hitch a ride. If one of the travelers is a queen, she can quickly form a colony when she gets to her destination. That's why there are Argentine ants living in the Nordic countries and European red ants in Australia.

Sometimes ants cause damage to their new environment, so we usually try to stop ants from spreading.

However, in 2014 a group of American pavement ants received permission to go on a long trip—to the International Space Station! Eight hundred ants lived in nests made out of plastic, while astronauts studied how they moved around without gravity.

Oh, I'm flying!

The farthest-traveled ant is the **PAVEMENT ANT**.

The ants survived the space journey. If humans ever went to live on another planet, you can be pretty sure that ants would follow along.

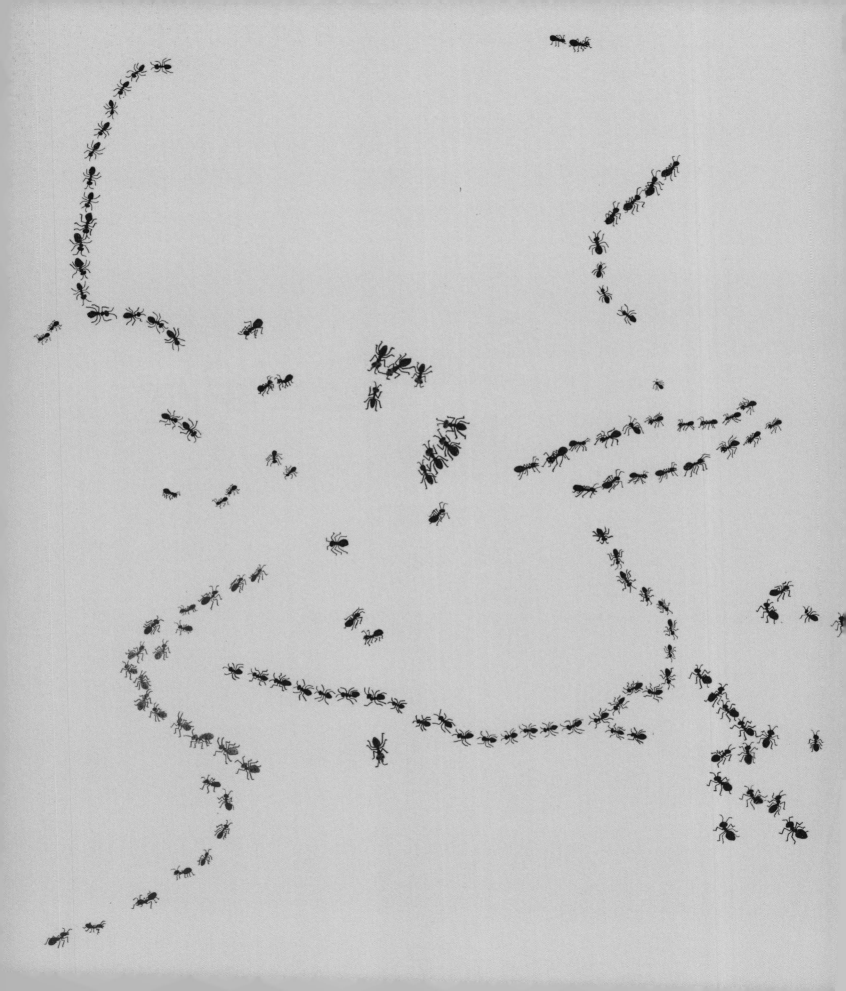

Index

adapting to the climate, 2, 36–37
American pavement ants, 40–41
ant colony
    largest, 8
    social organization, 9–11
anteaters, 34
antennae, 7
anthills
    getting home, 23
    temperature control, 36–37
    unwanted guests, 32
ant nests
    cleanest, 28–29
    new, 12–13, 27
    role of queen, 10, 13
    stealing of, 13
    temperature control, 36–37
    thatch roof, 16
ant population, worldwide, 4
ant trails, 6
aphids, farming of, 18
Azteca ant, 23–24

bears, 35
bites and stings, 14–15, 16
blue butterfly caterpillar, 32–33
bulldog ants, 15
bullet ants, 15

carpenter ants, 17, 30–31
communication, 6
cornfield ants, 17

defences
    bites and stings, 14–16, 30–31
    living doors, 30
desert ants, 2, 7, 22, 23
Dracula ants, 19

echidnas (spiny anteaters), 34
eggs, 10, 13

farming
    of aphids, 18
    of fungus, 26–27
female ants
    reproduction, 10–13
    workers, 9, 30–31, 39
fire ants, 15, 16
flying ants, 11, 12–13, 39
food
    aphid pee, 18
    fungus gardens, 26–27
    millipedes, 20
    a scent trail, 6
    strangest food, 19
foraging for food, 6, 23
formic acid, 15, 28
fungus gardens, 26–27

harvester ants, 15
health
    keeping clean, 28–29
    of queen, 10
honey bees, 15
humans
    eating of ants, 35
    strength and size, 25
    study of ants, 15, 29, 38
    take ants to space, 40–41

International Space Station, 40
invasive ant species, 40

jaws
    biting with, 6, 25
    carrying with, 6, 25
    and eating, 20
    of males, 11

ladybugs, 18
larvae, 19, 32, 35, 36
leafcutter ants, 26–27, 35
life cycle, 10, 13, 19, 35
life span, 38–39
living nests, 2

male ants, 11, 12, 39
millipedes, 20
mound ants
    clean nests, 28–29
    defences, 15
    a supercolony, 8
    with two homes, 25

narrow-headed ants, 38

pangolins (scaly anteaters), 34
pitchfork ants, 20–21
predators of ants, 32–35
princess ants
    of the leafcutter, 27, 35
    new nests, 11, 12–13
pupae, 35

queen ants
    largest, 17
    role of, 9, 13

rainforest ants, 30–31
red ants, 32, 40
reproduction, 10–13

sense of smell, 6–7
sense of taste, 6, 7
shiny sugar ants, 18, 29
social organization, 9–11
soldier ants, 30–31
space travel, 40–41
spider wasps, 15
stings and bites, 14–15, 16
superpowers
    angriest ant, 16
    and anthills, 8, 36–37
    cleanest ant, 29
    cleverest ant, 13
    and farming, 27
    fastest ant, 22, 23
    longest-lived ant, 38
    most frightening ant, 20
    sense of smell, 7
    sneakiest predator, 33

superpowers (*continued*)
    soldier ants, 30–31
    strangest food, 19
    strongest ant, 24, 25
    traveled to space, 40–41
    worst sting, 15
sweat bees, 15

temperature control, 36–37

venom of ants, 14, 31
vision, 7

weaver ants, 35
western thatching ants, 16
winged ants, 11, 12–13, 39
woodpeckers, 35
worker ants, 9, 30–31, 39
world ant population, 4–5
worldwide ants, 2–3, 40

yellow paper wasps, 15

Acknowledgments

Katja Bargum thanks Heikki Helanterä for his inspiring collaboration on the book *Myrornas hemliga liv* (*The secret lives of ants*), as well as the following organizations for their support: the Swedish Cultural Foundation in Finland, the Finnish Association of Science Editors and Journalists and the Association of Finnish Nonfiction Writers.

Jenny Lucander thanks her maternal grandfather, Harry Krogerus, for the inspiration, and the Finnish Cultural Foundation for the support.

This book was originally published in Swedish in Finland with support from the Delegation for the Promotion of Swedish Literature, which is administered by the Society of Swedish Literature in Finland.